Just for Kicks …
The American Presidents

by Wynn D. Day

Contents

- JIMMY CARTER (1977 - 1981)
- RONALD REAGAN (1981 - 1989)
- GEORGE BUSH SNR (1989 - 1993)
- BILL CLINTON (1993 - 2001)
- GEORGE W. BUSH (2001 - 2009)
- BARACK OBAMA (2009 - 2017)
- DONALD TRUMP (2017 - 2021)
- JOE BIDEN (2021 -)

George Washington (1789 - 1797)

George Washington was the first –

The one who broke the English curse.

A tall man, who on his horse he rode

At such speeds, he could explode.

He had false teeth upon a spring –

It was hard to eat anything.

The White House was not his home,

He was with Martha and was not alone.

John Adams (1797 - 1801)

John Adams wife was Abigail,

As wife and mother she did not fail.

He hoped the country would confirm

That he would be Prez for a second term.

But this guy they did not like,

So they told him 'to take a hike!'

Adams and Jefferson died on the same day,

When this dad died, for his son he made way.

Thomas Jefferson (1801 - 1809)

A great founding father was he,

Thomas Jefferson became number three.

He was very good at the written word,

And his constitution was forever heard.

Sally Hemings was his sister in law,

And with her he had six children more.

Throughout the world his fame has spread,

And carved on Mount Rushmore is his head.

James Madison (1809 - 1817)

Of the constitution, he was the father.

He got Louisiana but would rather

Organise the Democratic-Republican Party.

This was James Madison- quite a smarty.

Federalist papers with Alex Hamilton and John Jay.

His sponsorship of the Bill of Rights made the day.

The English burned the White House down,

But then they were chased out of town.

James Monroe (1817 - 1825)

Unpretentious and frank was James Monroe.

The Era of Good Feelings was his quid pro quo.

Also known as 'The Last Cocked Hat' –

Married to Elizabeth, so he didn't care about that.

No one stood against him from the other parties,

So with no opposition he was hale and hearty.

Maybe he didn't know what the Missouri Compromise was for

Cause it set the stage for the Civil War.

John Quincy Adams (1825 - 1829)

The first son of a president,

Off to the White House away Quincy went.

By mum Abigail he'd been taught,

He'd watched the Battle of Bunker Hill being fought.

The hatred of Andrew Jackson was his fate,

But he'd made a great Secretary of State.

He'd been efficient in lots of ways,

But it was a stroke that ended his days.

Andrew Jackson (1829 - 1837)

Old Hickory, Andrew Jackson loved cheese,

But it was he who left the Trail of Tears.

For taking land he saw no restriction,

And confirmed indigenous Indians eviction.

When it came to debt, he was not skittish,

At New Orleans he beat the British.

He killed a man in a duel,

And bashed another – he could be cruel.

Martin Van Buren (1837 - 1841)

It wasn't just a recession,

For Van Buren it was a depression.

Everything went really manic,

And in '37 caused the Great Panic.

He helped to create the Democrats,

But with John Calhoun there was combat.

When he had sailed to Europe,

His post in the senate Calhoun would stop.

William Henry Harrison (1841)

Mr Harrison – William Harry,

In the presidency he did not tarry.

He delivered his speech with no coat and hat,

But with impending pneumonia- he'd not thought about that.

He spent his month laid up in bed,

And after that – well he was dead.

Why he died was not a mystery.

It was the shortest term in history.

John Tyler (1841 - 1845)

John Tyler to the presidency did creep,

The first into the job after being veep.

Their slogan 'Tippee canoe and Tyler Too'

Made everyone question what he could do.

He vetoed bills and raised tariff rates,

But his worthiness is open to debate.

He has a grandson now still living,

So his legacy keeps giving.

James Polk (1845 - 1849)

The extension of territory was Polk's gift,

To create the United States and lift

The country to become a world power,

A dark horse candidate, he won the hour.

He achieved all things on his agenda,

After one term his presidency was for surrender.

He went to Tennessee to abide,

And three months later there he died.

Zachary Taylor (1849 - 1850)

Zachary Taylor – old rough and ready,

With a tiny majority he was unsteady.

With no prior practical experience

His few achievements were no coincidence.

As major general in the war with Mexico,

He dealt their forces a crushing blow.

He managed sixteen months in office,

Then Millard Fillmore took over this.

Millard Fillmore (1850 - 1853)

Millard Fillmore and his opponent Weed,

Jinxed him in office when he to tried to succeed.

Men waited for Taylor's death at Hotel Willard,

When the presidency was awarded to Millard.

Slavery divided them and against their wills

Millard divided the compromise into five bills.

His wife and daughter died within a year.

His life after office held little cheer.

Franklin Pierce (1853 - 1857)

Pierce's time in office was to suck,

His life became blighted with bad luck.

All his three sons died very young,

His wife was certain his presidency was wrong.

Problems with wife and country would double,

And through congress there was only trouble.

As an alcoholic his life would end,

It must have seemed he had no friend.

James Buchanan (1857 - 1861)

James Buchanan said to be the worst,

But his pres was undoubtedly cursed.

The last one before the Civil War

That would sear the country to the core.

At the White House he bred pigmy goats,

He may have been gay – it is wrote.

Still they were glad when he was gone,

So Abe Lincoln could get the war won.

Abraham Lincoln (1861 - 1865)

Abe Lincoln of all was said to be best,

The Civil War was his greatest test.

The nation in trouble, he wondered whether

He could abolish slavery and bring things back together.

After the war when things became smooth,

He had an encounter with John Wilkes Booth.

The theatre invitation that he had got,

Was where he took his final shot.

Andrew Johnson (1865 - 1869)

To cure the country if he can –

But Andrew Johnson was not the man.

He'd not been taught to read and write,

And vetoed bills by day and night.

And through the government conflict grew,

As his impeachment began to brew.

His hopelessness could not have been greater.

He was widely regarded as a traitor.

Ulysses S. Grant (1869 - 1877)

Andrew Johnson was viewed as defective,

While Ulysses Grant was thought effective.

Though through the Civil War he'd won –

He had to have his meat well done.

And in the war with his forces,

He showed his great skill with horses.

Then at 63 to his maker he went,

His wife with a squint was Julia Boggs Dent.

Rutherford B. Hayes (1877 - 1881)

Then we had Rutherford B. Hayes,

With wife 'Lemonade Lucy' whose ways

Heralded simplicity and good sense.

When his election had caused offence,

The dispute called the 'Tilden-Hayes' affair

Resulted in 'His fraudulency' being his care.

So to one term he did concede,

The voice of the electorate he would heed.

James Garfield (March 1881 - Sept 1881)

James Garfield comes in at number twenty,

As for cleverness – he had plenty.

He said he didn't know how to swim,

But at the canal, 16 times he fell in.

After four months into his time,

Guiteau came and committed his crime.

Poor Garfield got a real bad deal,

With a septic wound that would not heal.

Chester Arthur (1881 - 1885)

Chester Arthur was given the invitation,

Upon James Garfield's assassination,

To step up from being the veep,

He had eighty pairs of trousers to keep.

Twas said he found being pres hard,

And was wounded by folks' low regard.

But upon the sea so wavy,

He modernised the American navy.

Grover Cleveland (1885 - 89 & 1893 - 97)

Grover Cleveland was twenty two and twenty four,

The people liked him- so he came back for more!

"Hey ma, where's my pa? Gone to the White House, ha ha ha"

The illegitimate child claims were not bizarre.

This event caused quite a scandal,

But it wasn't too big for him to handle.

In the White House to Frances he was married,

But his re-election was not carried.

Benjamin Harrison (1889 - 1893)

Of William Henry, his grandson Ben,

He was elected in 1889 when –

In Indiana there was voter fraud,

So he won the presidency with that accord.

After he had helped in the Civil War,

He decided to go into Law.

He was judged by the people to be cold,

And died when he was 67 years old.

Grover Cleveland (1893 - 1897)

When Grover returned in ninety three,

It wasn't how he wanted it to be.

He said the economy was ruined by Ben.

It was the depression and panic when

He wanted to change the silver in coins.

The people won't have it-it was purloined!

And with Maria Halpin on his case,

He left office with her to face.

William McKinley (1897 - 1901)

Just to help him win the hour,

For luck, McKinley would don a red flower.

So when he ran for a second term,

He was liked, so it was affirmed.

How it would end, no one prophesied.

His two children in infancy died.

To a little girl he handed his red carnation,

To set the stage for his assassination.

Theodore Roosevelt (1901 - 1909)

Theodore got a presidency he didn't expect,

And at first there was not much respect.

His wife and mother died on the same day,

So to the Wild West he went away.

He was shot while giving a speech,

But with the Panama Canal built he was a peach!

When this gas bag was let loose,

He formed the party of the Bull Moose.

William Howard Taft (1909 - 1913)

Taft was real big friends with Teddy,

Who ordained him to be next, but was he ready?

Taft, as president, didn't much care for that,

He was so uncomfortable – he grew fat!

He cared for wife Nell when she had a stroke.

He "was boring-honest, likeable, but boring" I quote.

He became Chief Justice of the Supreme Court,

It was his dream – and for this he was well thought.

Woodrow Wilson (1913 - 1921)

All because of Teddy's and Bill Taft's feud,

Woodrow Wilson won next, he was clever and shrewd.

During World War One his dream creation

Was to set up the United Nations.

While out campaigning a stroke meant no more speech,

And wife Edith then stepped into the breach.

The first First Lady to run the show,

As history has revealed – that's how we know!

Warren Harding (1921 - 1923)

Warren Harding was number twenty nine.

There were lots of scandals in his time.

The Teapot Dome was a headliner,

He gambled away the White House china!

He had a daughter with Nan Britton,

He's one of the worst presidents, it is written.

After two years in office he died,

But an autopsy was never tried.

Calvin Coolidge (1923 - 1929)

Calvin Coolidge was negative and remote.

He did nothing and left the economy to float.

Of the country he said; 'A state of contentment seldom before seen.'

He continued in nothingness, but was serene.

A depression in waiting is what they'd get,

While Rebecca the racoon was his pet.

The 'fine personal influence' of his wife Grace

At least gave his presidency a pleasant face.

Herbert Hoover (1929 - 1933)

Herbert Hoover was the next one who ran,

Everything was good when he began.

Then they all ran out of cash,

And they had the Wall Street Crash.

And poor Herbert with his commendable history,

Could not conquer the depression mystery.

Then came the time of the Hoover Villes,

When he was gone they were there still.

Franklin D. Roosevelt (1933 - 1945)

Then to cure Hoover's sin,

We had Eleanor and Franklin.

The wheelchair pres of four terms,

The troubles were hard to fix he would learn.

When Eleanor found the letters of Lucy Mercer,

Franklin had good reason to curse her.

With fireside chats and nuclear bombs,

People were devastated when he was gone.

Harry S. Truman (1945 - 1953)

When Harry came to sort the trouble

Hiroshima was to burst the bubble.

That was the end of World War two,

And the Charter of the United Nations was due.

For Western Europe his Marshall Plan,

And creating NATO – he was the man.

The squirrels at the White House he would feed.

He was a good pres – it was agreed.

Dwight Eisenhower (1953 - 1961)

With banners proclaiming 'I like Ike!'

And because he'd been General and warlike,

He'd been asked to run for President.

He didn't want it – but did relent.

During the war, in those days

Very close to him was his sweet driver Kay.

He set up the war in Vietnam,

He didn't do much else – a bit of a sham!

John F. Kennedy (1961 - 1963)

JFK – pres of a thousand days,

With lovely family and winning ways.

And many women like Judith and Marilyn,

Very oversexed – that was his sin!

The Cuban Missile Crisis and Bay of Pigs

Enhanced his reputation to very big.

With Lee Harvey Oswald waiting in Dallas,

He spent his last day there – alas!

Lyndon B. Johnson (1963 - 1969)

Sworn in on Airforce One,

Johnson's troublesome presidency begun.

Left the legacy of the Vietnam War,

Throughout his time it was a running sore.

While the young all started tripping,

He'd hold meetings while skinny dipping.

He was known with his dog to howl,

But overall, his time in office fell fowl.

Richard Nixon (1969 - 1974)

The tone was lowered by Tricky Dicky,

Whose time as pres proved very sticky.

'Would you buy a used car from this man?'

Burgling the Watergate Building was his plan.

Cover ups and bungling was how he'd play,

Spying on the Democrats was his way.

He spread his arms as if crucified,

Proposed impeachment the reward for his lies.

Gerald Ford (1974 - 1977)

So the way for Gerald Ford was erected,

He was the pres who was never elected.

Two assassination attempts on his life,

But he seems to have been famous for his wife.

Good old Betty with her clinic,

But for pardoning Nixon he was judged to be thick.

He was known for falling down,

After one short term, he left town.

Jimmy Carter (1977 - 1981)

Jimmy Carter was a farmer of the nut,

A total unknown to start with but

He had big problems with Iran,

The hostage crisis was bigger than

Anything else during his time,

The helicopter crash became a shrine.

He continued to look increasingly weak,

But his life after was not bleak.

Ronald Reagan (1981 - 1989)

Ron Reagan straight from Hollywood,

He turned out to be quite good.

He brought back prosperity and pride,

Every challenge he took in his stride.

He met Russian leader Gorbachov,

And John Hinckley – he saw him off.

Reagan was known as one of the greats,

But dementia was waiting – it was his fate.

George Bush Snr (1989 - 1993)

George Bush Senior moved into the dock,

Previously known as an 'overwound cuckoo clock'.

He sorted out the first Gulf war,

But left Saddam which invited more

Action-later. To expand influence across the map

He threw up in Japanese PMs lap.

When he finally lost his grip

Was when he said, "Read my lips."

Bill Clinton (1993 - 2001)

Bill and Hillary came in next,

But this guy sure was oversexed.

With Gennifer, Paula and Monica's dress,

He excelled at the caress.

People became fed up with this double-

Always persecuted, always in trouble.

With his eye off the ball to sort the drama,

He should have been seeing to Osama.

George W. Bush (2001 - 2009)

Georgie Bush could not string a sentence together,

But he bombed Iraq and didn't care whether

He smashed their country and ruined their culture,

He sure can be likened to a vulture.

He blamed all this on the fall of the towers,

But this guy should never have been given the power.

Maybe Cheney was his task master,

And helped contribute to this disaster.

Barack Obama (2009 - 2017)

Then we had Mr Nice Guy Obama,

He was the one who killed Osama.

He gave the presidency a touch of class,

On election day he put Hillary out to grass.

There seemed to be a lot of golf to play,

And he seemed to do it every day.

At the end of his time there was a big bump.

He had to make way for Donald Trump.

Donald Trump (2017 - 2021)

Sad to say they elected a chump,

By the name of Donald Trump.

He put his propaganda on Twitter,

And the electorate grew increasingly bitter.

Unaccountable, rumbustious and outspoken,

Anarchy spreading – the country broken.

On the Capitol building he encouraged attack,

And still he threatens to come back!

Joe Biden (2021 -)

After Trump they need someone tame,

So then along Joe Biden came.

The oldest elected pres by far,

But after Trump anyone would be a star.

He seems to find the job quite hard,

And reads his speeches from a card.

But he's still going and doing the biz,

So at the moment the presidency is his.

Printed in Great Britain
by Amazon

ISBN 9798372728455